INVISIBLE MARKETING

Discover the Missing Piece in Your Marketing Strategy to
Build Loyalty, Influence and Repeat Business

INVISIBLE MARKETING

Discover the Missing Piece in Your Marketing Strategy to Build Loyalty, Influence and Repeat Business

SANJEEV BUDHIRAJA

Available on amazonkindle

Worldwide Published by

Pendown Press
PREMIUM BUSINESS PUBLISHER

PENDOWN PRESS LLP

An ISO 9001 & ISO 14001 Certified Co.,

Regd. Office: 3767A, Kanhaiya Nagar,
Tri Nagar, Delhi-110035

Ph.: 8130886000, 9650072927

E-mail: info@pendownpress.com

Branch Office: 1A/2A, 20, Hari Sadan, Ansari Road,
Daryaganj, New Delhi-110002

Ph.: 011-45794768

Website: PendownPress.com

Edition: 2025

Price: ₹ 299

ISBN: 978-93-6338-269-5

Layout and Cover Designed by Pendown Graphics Team

Printed and Bound in India by Thomson Press India Ltd.

Table of Contents

Chapter 1

THE STORY BEHIND THIS BOOK

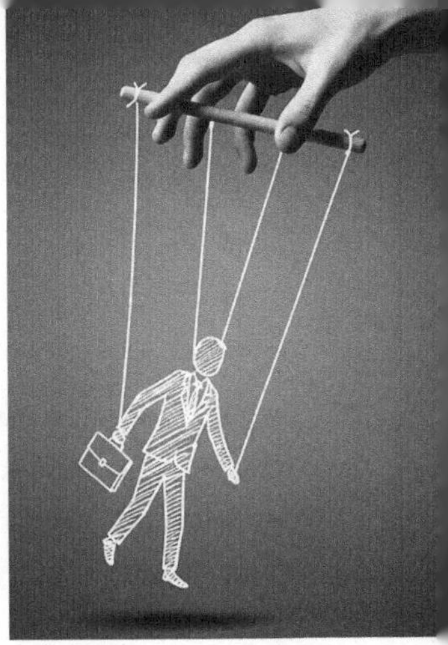

In 1995, during my engineering at S.L.I.E.T, one evening I was walking through the college campus, I saw a girl and felt an instant connection—something I couldn't explain. I was a very shy person, but a few days later, I gathered enough courage to reach out to her.

I soon realized it was a one-sided feeling. She didn't feel the same.

It broke my heart. For a few months, I was emotionally shattered. I slipped into a phase of deep sadness and loneliness. I tried to come out of it, but I could not. Then I met my first mentor, who came from Canada to India to develop a network marketing business. He taught me many things and suggested that I read self-development books.

I began reading—and that's when I discovered some powerful ideas: the achievement process, the law of attraction, the power of spoken words & the power of the **subconscious mind.**

That heartbreak became the turning point of my life. I read hundreds of books and started practicing those laws. Those laws were not just theory.

Nine years later, I married the same girl, against all odds!

I used the same principles to manifest my dream home and the freedom of time and money in my business. I even manifested international travel to 11 countries in 2024. Later in this book, I'll reveal the exact secret I learned to create my desired reality with the power of spoken words and a belief-shifting method.

In 2021, I started learning marketing to implement the marketing strategies for my business. This learning and the implementation continued for more than 4 years. In 2024, I found that I could blend the marketing strategies with the belief-shifting method I had learned in my college. This blending of proven marketing strategies with my experiential learning of belief shifting gave birth to Invisible Marketing.

With Invisible Marketing, you do not chase the customers. Rather, you attract the customers, not by manipulation, but by resonance. When you apply Invisible Marketing strategies to your business, you don't have to "push" people to buy from you. They naturally gravitate toward you, trust you, and choose you.

In this book, I will reveal exactly how you can master Invisible Marketing to create unstoppable growth — both in your personal life and in your business.

Whether you are a business owner or a coach, or a professional, this book will show you a very clear path to be remembered, referred and respected by your customers. You will discover a step-by-step, clear path to exponential growth in this book.

It will show you the science and strategies that work invisibly to change your customers' beliefs and perceptions & make them your fan in less than 3 months. Invisible Marketing is the shortest & cheapest way to make your customers repeatedly buy from you and give you referrals without even asking for it.

Here's what you'll discover inside this book:

If You're a Business Owner...

- You'll discover how to **shift the beliefs** of your customers, so they don't just buy once, they buy again and again.
- You'll learn the **invisible process of gaining trust & respect** that gets you **referrals and repeat orders without asking**.
- You'll know exactly how to **create "Wow" moments** in your customer journey that **position you as premium**, without reducing price.

If You're a Professional or Freelancer...

- You'll discover how to make clients **remember you, refer you, and rave about you**—even when you're not in the room.
- You'll stop "following up" and start creating **pull-based relationships** that feel natural and frictionless.
- You'll learn how to build your personal brand through small, thoughtful, high-impact touchpoints.

If You're a Coach, Trainer, or Consultant...

- You'll see how to **anchor your teachings** in the mind of your clients, so they remember and apply them every day.
- How to make your teachings tangible and memorable, so they get implemented.
- You'll install a system that increases **retention, referrals, and renewals**—automatically.

By Learning the Invisible Marketing Framework, You'll Be Able To...

- Design **buying experiences** that trigger respect, loyalty, and advocacy

- Turn customer touchpoints into **WOW experiences**
- Create a **magnetic brand** that people talk about and trust
- Build a **referral machine** without asking
- **Make your business unforgettable**—in the most subtle, strategic way possible

Chapter 2

BELIEFS THAT DRIVE SALES

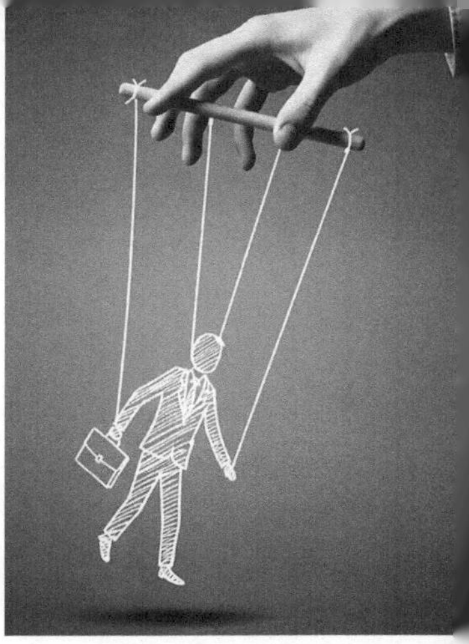

In 2021, I was striving to increase my income & profitability. Since an increase in profitability is directly related to an increase in sales, I was doing all these things to increase sales in my business....

- Adding more products
- Joining networking groups
- Hiring more salespeople
- Giving discounts & offers to customers
- Burning money in digital ads to generate more leads
- Sending Bulk WhatsApp on Data

Despite doing all the above things, my business seemed stagnant.

Then, a friend of mine referred me to attend a masterclass on marketing by Akshar Yadav. After attending that class, my belief shifted, and I came to know that the real reason for stagnation is that I have no marketing strategy to differentiate my products in the market.

I learned that Marketing is not just visibility, Marketing is changing your customers' beliefs to create the buying environment, which makes your sales easy or automatic.

Before your customers buy your product, they must believe in these 4 things

- Believe that they have the problem. If they don't feel the pain, they don't feel the need.
- Believe that you have the solution to their problem.
- Believe that you and your company are trustworthy.
- Believe that it's the right time for them to buy the solution you are offering.

What Drove Your Decision?

Imagine a potential customer who likes your products and says,

"Let me think about it."

"Not right now."

"Will get back to you."

If this happens to you, all you need to do is fix your marketing.

The purpose of marketing is—

1. To help them discover their pain and problems.
2. To show how your product solves the problem.
3. To show social proof & your story to make them trust you.
4. To show them what they lose by not buying now.

When you do marketing to change the beliefs of customers, you create an environment in which customers are eager to buy.

Let's do a small exercise…

Think of the moment when you purchased your car, what beliefs of the salesperson or marketing of the car brand shifted in your mind before you gave the cheque to the car salesperson?

> Think of a moment when you did not buy something because the salesperson or the company was unable to shift your beliefs that were required to make the buying decision.
>
> **Just like your beliefs are shaping your buying decisions, your customers also buy when they believe in certain things about you, your products, their need, and their urgency.**

If you are facing problems like declining profitability or sales, it's just a symptom; the root cause may be - your customers do not believe in you or your offerings, or they believe that they do not need your product or do not need it at the moment.

In this situation, if you keep on chasing your customers & try to drive sales with discounts and offers. It's like when you have a stomach infection, you keep on consuming painkillers when you really need antibiotics to cure the problem at the root.

Similarly, declining sales in business is the symptom & when you do not know the root cause & work on symptoms, you lose your prime time and get frustrated.

Knowing the root cause is 50% of the solution, and the remaining 50% is taking action to solve the root cause.

The root cause of declining sales or profitability is lousy marketing or selling without marketing.

Look at it like this ...

Sales is just a transaction, & marketing builds the trust, belief, and desire in your customer's mind to do that transaction.

When you fix the marketing ...

- You do not chase customers —they come with curiosity.
- You do not convince customers —they already believe.
- You do not give discounts —they see the value.

Your financial growth is one of the major purposes of your business. For your business growth, you need more sales, and to have more sales, you need the right marketing. If your product is good and your business is still not growing, Marketing is the missing link. Marketing is not an expense, it's the best investment you can make to boost your sales and profit. In the next chapter, you will understand what marketing is and how you can make the blueprint for marketing in your organization.

⦸⦸⦸⦸

Chapter 3

THE MARKETING BLUEPRINT

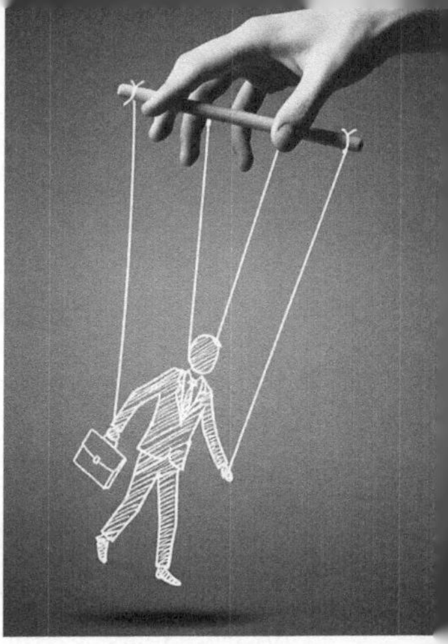

3 Elements of Marketing

Dan Kennedy, in his book Magnetic Marketing, explains the 3 elements of marketing, which are also widely known as the **"Golden Triangle of Marketing"**. One of my mentors & friend, Akshar Yadav, who is a master marketer, emphasizes that **"Marketing fails because one of the triangle sides is weak."**

Right Message to the Right Market via Right Media = Conversions

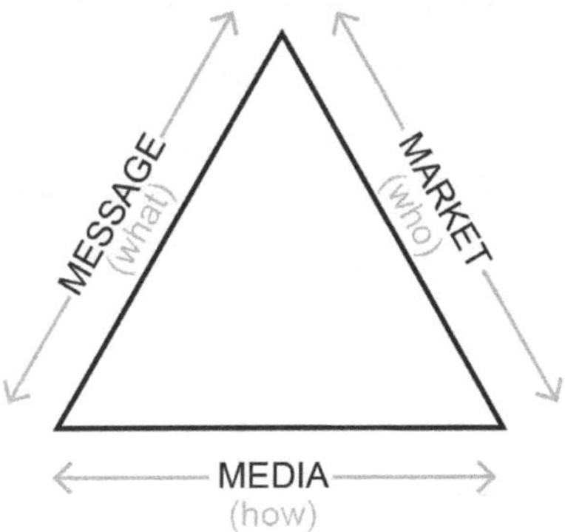

1. Market – Who are you targeting - (your ideal customer)?

The most important component in any marketing is the market. You can have the best copy, the best offer, and still fail if you're aiming at the wrong people. So, creating your ideal customer profile is the first and most critical step. Write your ideal customers' demographics & psychographics. Meet your ideal customers and know their needs, desires, fears & frustrations.

2. Message – What belief do you want to shift or build in them?

Your message must match the market's mindset. It must address their needs, desires, fears, and frustrations. Your message and offers must be emotionally and logically aligned with what the market already believes or desires. Craft messages for belief-shifting, transforming skepticism into trust through persuasive storytelling, guarantees, and testimonials.

3. Media – How will you give that message (Email, WhatsApp, ads, Webinars, etc.)?

It doesn't matter how great your ad is if it's in the wrong place. Selecting the right media (Facebook, email, print, direct mail, etc.) is essential to ensure your message reaches your market. You can test multiple channels till you find what's working best for your market.

The Market - The 1st Element of the Marketing Triangle

It's very important to understand the psychology of your ideal customer. Customers' awareness and beliefs are dynamically changing during the buying process. By meeting your ideal customers, you discover their demographics & psychographics. You become aware of their needs, desires, fears & frustrations. You will observe the mindset shifts that the customer goes through in the buying process. This we call as Buyer Journey or Customer Journey

At each stage in the customer journey, your job is to create the required amount of belief in your customer's mind so that buying becomes obvious. If you understand these stages of awareness that the customer goes through while buying your product, you can control the flow and create the buying environment for your customer

Eugene M. Schwartz, in his legendary book Breakthrough Advertising, introduced this classic marketing framework called ...

The 5 Stages of Awareness

Customers go through the 5 stages of awareness while buying any product. Does not matter what your business is, in each business, customers go through these 5 stages of awareness.

Only by understanding these 5 stages of awareness in your customer's journey can you master the art and science of marketing.

1. Unaware: When a customer is not aware of the problem, or they won't admit it.

2. Problem Aware: When a customer realises that they have a problem, but don't know how to solve it.

3. Solution Aware: When customers know solutions exist, but not specific products.

4. **Product Aware:** When customers know your product exists, but don't fully understand it, or trust it yet.

5. **Most Aware:** When customers know and like your product, but have not purchased it yet.

The Message - The 2nd Element of the Marketing Triangle

Schwartz was a master marketer who had a hit ratio of 85% (percentage of winning ads), which is one of the highest in copywriting history. His framework is foundational in crafting messages that lead to conversions

This framework can help you to match your message to the customer's current mindset—a core principle in belief-shifting marketing used by top brands. The table below has 5 stages of awareness that your customer goes through step by step. You need to understand the customer's mindset at each level of awareness, what your goal should be & which marketing strategy you should use at that stage of awareness.

AWARENESS STAGE	CURRENT BELIEF OF CUSTOMER	YOUR INTENTION	YOUR MARKETING TACTIC	NEW BELIEF OF CUSTOMER
Unaware	I don't have a problem.	Spark curiosity	Storytelling, emotional hooks, and hidden pain	Maybe something's missing in my life/business
Problem Aware	Something feels off.	Agitate the problem	Show consequences, amplify the pain	This needs to be fixed now
Solution Aware	There must be a fix.	Educate	Explain the types of solutions, and become their guide	This type of solution can help me
Product Aware	I've seen your product... not convinced.	Build trust	Share proof, features, and differentiation	This one is different and right for me
Most Aware	I like it... haven't bought it yet.	Drive action	Add urgency, offers, risk reversal, and CTA	Now is the best time to act

Using the above framework, your marketing message will be targeted to shift your customers' beliefs to take them to the next stage of the customer journey. Your all marketing collaterals like ads, emails, phone conversations, website, WhatsApp messages, catalogs, webinars, 1-2-1 meetings, promotional gifts, etc, will become belief-shifting tools. Once you know the science and art of shifting your customer's belief, sales is a byproduct. It's automatic and easy.

Media - The 3rd Element Of Marketing Triangle

Media refers to the channels used to deliver your marketing message to the market (the target audience)

There are 2 kinds of Media

- **Online Media**: Facebook ads, Instagram Reels, Google search, WhatsApp, YouTube, Email
- **Offline Media**: Events, meetings, exhibitions, print ads, in-store displays, gifting merchandise.

The right message sent to the right market on the wrong media = wasted money.

Ask yourself:

- Where is your audience already paying attention?
- Which media builds trust and visibility the fastest for your niche?
- Are you matching the media to the psychology of your customer's buying state?

MARKET + MESSAGE + MEDIA = TOUCHPOINT

When your customer interacts with your brand via online or offline media, a touchpoint is created. Every Touchpoint is an opportunity to do marketing. Throughout the customer journey at all 5 stages of awareness, your customer is interacting with your brand via various online and offline channels. Every touchpoint is either weakening or strengthening your brand's positioning. Your job is to align your marketing message with your customers' awareness stage at every touchpoint. This way, you get your customers' attention, shift their beliefs, and sell easily.

Effective Marketing is controlling–

- How and when your customer will interact with your business to create touchpoints
- Engineering the belief-shifting marketing messages and tools at all touch-points in your customer's buying journey.
- A well-designed customer-buying journey will give you their attention & shift their beliefs to drive conversion.

Example of a touchpoint in the journey of a 40-year-old business owner buying a Luxury Car

- **Market:** A 40-year-old business owner looking to buy a luxury car, not just for commuting, but as a statement of success.
- **Message:** "This isn't just a car. It's proof you've arrived."
- **Media:** Instagram Reel showing the car gliding through a city skyline with the quote, "You don't chase success. You drive it."

The purpose of this touch-point is to make him call the car dealership for more details & that call will be the next touch-point in his buying journey, followed by a demo of the car and eventually owning the car and advocating the brand to the market.

Marketing isn't random content. It's the engineering of belief-shifting touchpoints in your customers' buying journey. If you get your Market, Message, and Media right at all the touch-points, you create the irresistible desire in your customer's mind to buy your product.

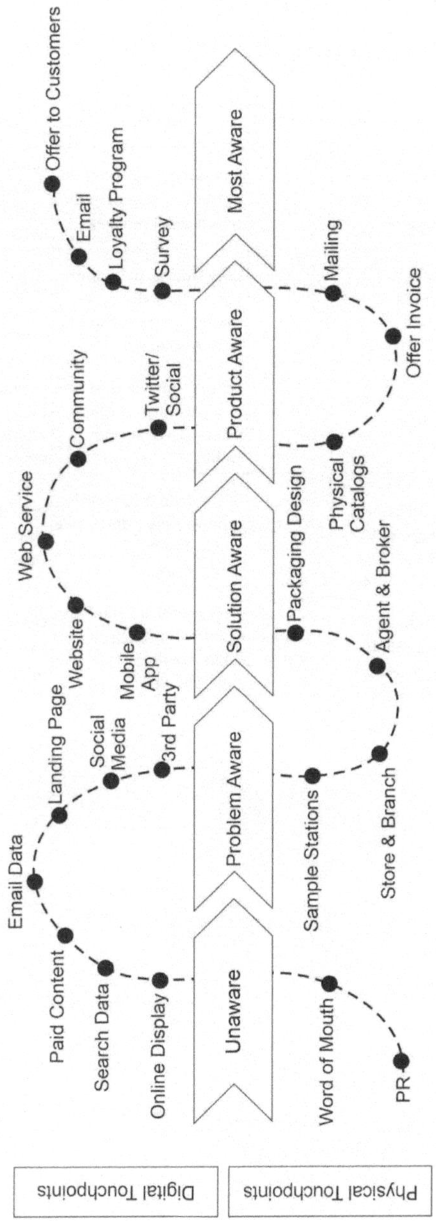
Unaware
Problem Aware
Solution Aware
Product Aware
Most Aware
Online Display
Search Data
Paid Content
Email Data
Landing Page
Social Media
3rd Party
Mobile App
Website
Web Service
Community
Twitter/ Social
Survey
Loyalty Program
Email
Offer to Customers
PR
Word of Mouth
Sample Stations
Store & Branch
Agent & Broker
Packaging Design
Physical Catalogs
Offer Invoice
Mailing
Digital Touchpoints
Physical Touchpoints

B2b Business: Touch-Points in a Customer Journey

Stage	Customer Mindset	Your Goal	Strategy	Key Touchpoints
Unaware	"I don't even realize something is slowing down my growth."	Spark curiosity	Use storytelling, LinkedIn content, or questions that reflect silent problems	LinkedIn posts, Trade show conversations, Vox calls, Cold email with insight hook
Problem Aware	"Something's broken—but I don't know the root cause."	Agitate the problem	Case studies, pain-centric narratives, industry trends that reveal hidden costs of inaction	LinkedIn carousels, Blogs, Discovery calls, Lead magnets
Solution Aware	"We need to fix this. What are the options?"	Educate & guide	Teach frameworks, show how others are solving it, value-based blueprints, webinars	Long-form video, Webinars, 1–2–1 meetings, WhatsApp/email education series
Product Aware	"Your offer sounds promising—will it work for us?"	Build trust & de-risk	Share deep testimonials, remove risks, side-by-side and competitor comparisons	Personalized demos, Proposal decks, Use-case videos, Sales calls
Most Aware	"I'm almost convinced. Should I act now or later?"	Trigger decision	Remove risk (guarantees, bonuses), add urgency, limited seats, pricing tiers, strong CTA	Follow-up calls, Deadline-based emails, WhatsApp reminders, Final pitch decks

D2c Business: Touch-Points in a Customer Journey

Stage	Customer Mindset	Your Goal	Strategy	Key Touchpoints
Unaware	I don't even know I need something like this	Create emotional curiosity	Inspiring reels, transformation-led content, emotion-led storytelling	Instagram Reels,YouTube Shorts, Tik Tok, Viral Stories
Problem Aware	I'm frustrated or unfulfilled, but not sure what can help.	Connect to their hidden frustrations or desires	Pain/pleasure hooks, day-in-the-life problems, lifestyle resonance	Carousel posts, Nurture emails, Blog articles, WhatsApp educational messages
Solution Aware	I'm exploring solutions to feel better, do better, or live better.	Show how your product solves that feeling	Before-after comparisons, user journeys, solution -focused content	Product pages, Explainer videos, Testimonials, Live sessions
Product Aware	Your product looks interesting-does it really work for people like me?	Prove It works and make it feel relatable	UGC, reviews, influencer validation, demo videos, use cases	Review sections, Instagram Stories, highlighted customer feedback
Most Aware	I just need a push- should buy this now or wait?	Drive urgency or fear of missing out	Time-sensitive offers, bundle deals, cart reminders, urgency CTAS	WhatsApp Messages, Offer popups, email retargeting, Abandoned cart flows

Retail Business: Touch-Points in a Customer Journey

Stage	Customer Mindset	Your Goal	Strategy	Key Touchpoints
Unaware	I'm just browsing—I don't have a need in mind.	Grab visual attention	Attractive window displays, eye-catching packaging, and impulse visuals	Storefront signage, POP displays, in-store screens, and flyers
Problem Aware	I wish my experience (home, gifting, look, etc.) felt better.	Trigger a lifestyle emotion or need	Live demos, shelf talkers, in-store videos, and relatable messaging	Sales staff engagement, sample stations, demo counters
Solution Aware	I'm open to finding something that suits my taste or need.	Present the product as the perfect fit	Showcase benefits, use visuals that show results, taste/test trials	Shelf branding, packaging design, and in-store influencer endorsements
Product Aware	This product looks good, but should I get it from this store?	Build trust and preference	Customer reviews, quality assurance, loyalty programs	Customer testimonials in-store, loyalty apps, and physical catalogs
Most Aware	I like it. Should I buy it now or wait for a better offer?	Convert with urgency or value	Limited-time discounts, in-store offers, combo deals	Cash counter offers, SMS reminders, WhatsApp store alerts

Coaching Business: Touch-Points in a Customer Journey

Stage	Customer Mindset	Your Goal	Strategy	Key Touchpoints
Unaware	I'm stuck, but I don't know if coaching can help.	Create identity -based curiosity	Relatable stories, belief-shifting posts, polarizing reels	Instagram Reels, Podcast clips, YouTube, Meta ads
Problem Aware	I know I'm facing a challenge, but unsure how to fix it.	Reveal emotional pain or aspirations	Pain-point content, self-doubt triggers, mirror moments	Email sequences, Carousel posts, Free PDF guides, Self-assessment quizzes
Solution Aware	I'm exploring ways to improve—coaching might be one.	Position coaching as the bridge to results	Explain your method, share client breakthroughs, and teach frameworks	Free masterclasses, Live Q&As, Coaching framework posts, WhatsApp nurture flows
Product Aware	I've heard of your program—is it right for me?	Show how your coaching uniquely delivers	Social proof, niche positioning, behind-the-scenes of coaching	Client success reels, Before-and-after interviews, Case study videos, DM conversations
Most Aware	I'm ready to commit —but is now the right time?	Push commitment through trust and urgency	Bonuses, deadlines, testimonials, commitment-framing content	Final-day emails, Limited seats WhatsApp, Free call CTA, Urgency-based stories

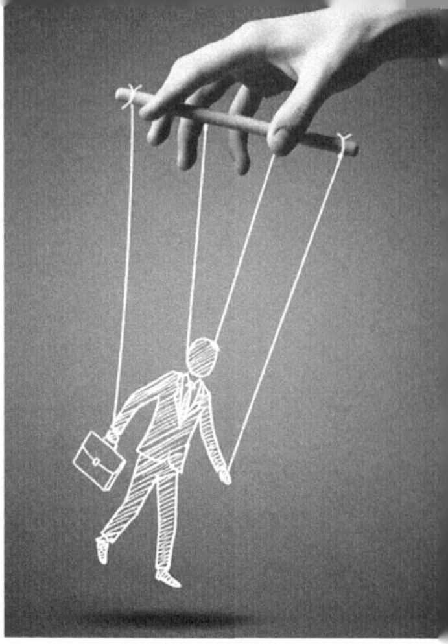

Chapter 4

GOING AN EXTRA MILE IN MARKETING

Going an extra mile means doing more than what is expected, not because you have to, but because you choose to. It's a mindset of going beyond average, beyond obligation, and creating extraordinary value, effort, or experience.

Educating customers in their buying journey is the core hygiene of any business that you must do, but helping customers to fulfill their purpose behind buying the product is going the extra mile. If you help and contribute to the success journey of your customer, it goes an extra mile. You go the extra mile when you become useful to your customers in achieving their goal.

Just Do IT!

If you look at truly successful companies, they don't do marketing just to sell products — they inspire transformation.

They become partners in their customers' journey to win.

- For example, Nike does not say, "Buy our product." Rather, it says-"You're capable of more — and we're here to help you unlock it."

- Nike inspires customers to find the greatness inside them. Nike celebrates customer stories — disabled athletes, underdogs, late bloomers — showing them what's possible.
- Nike links their brand with empowering words – "Just Do It".

In my manifestation journey, I learned that whatever is repeated in the mind becomes a mantra for the mind. With repetition, it starts rewiring the brain, and when a brand is associated with that positive mantra, it is remembered and respected.

Apple is marketing by anchoring its brand to a bigger mission. Apple links its brand with empowering words – "Think Different."Apple says Creative rebels change the world & inspire their customers to have creativity, dreams & vision. They showcase user-generated innovation — filmmakers, designers, students.

➢ **Notion is another company that encourages customers to organize their lives**. The company teaches the users how to use Notion to achieve personal goals.

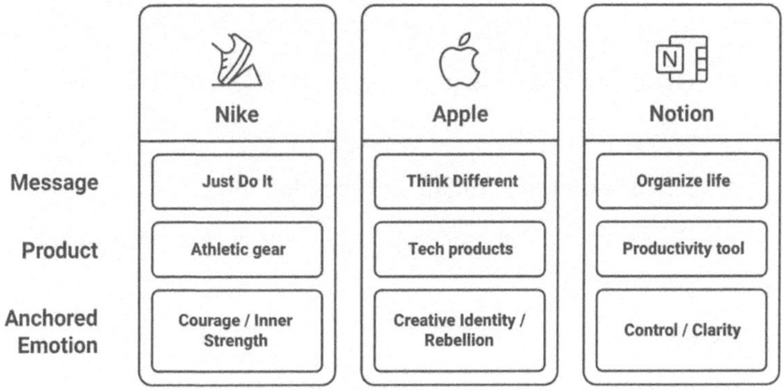

- What does your customer think when they see your brand?
- Do you want to link your brand with positivity just like Nike, Apple & Notion?
- Are you willing to go the extra mile in marketing?

How can you go the extra mile in your marketing? How can you inspire your customer to succeed?

During my college, when I started reading self-improvement books, the first thing I learned was the 5-Step Achievement Process. The 5-step achievement process is the same for me, you, and as well as your customers. Going the extra mile is being useful to your customer in their achievements.

Here is the 5-Step Achievement Process

1. **Desires & Dreams**
   - The starting point — your vision, what you truly want
   - Bible Says - without vision, people perish
2. **Goals**
   - A goal is a dream with a date on it and a deadline to achieve it.
   - Defining clear, measurable goals is necessary to succeed.
3. **Planning**
   - People don't plan to fail, but they fail to plan.
   - Breaking the longer journey into visible milestones is planning.
4. **Belief**
   - Believe and you are halfway there.
   - Building strong internal conviction that you can & you will achieve it.

5. **Action**

- One of my mentors gave me a 2-step formula for success - **Just Start & Don't Quit**
- Taking relentless, focused steps until you reach the outcome

Inspiring your customer in their achievement process is surely an extra mile you must go while marketing at touchpoints. If you help your customer win, your winning is inevitable. In your customer journey at various touchpoints, when you inspire your customer, your brand becomes a part of their success journey. Not only does selling become obvious, but you will be respected and referred for your usefulness beyond the transaction. In Next Chapter will reveal the secret strategy that will make your business growth transformational instead of transactional.

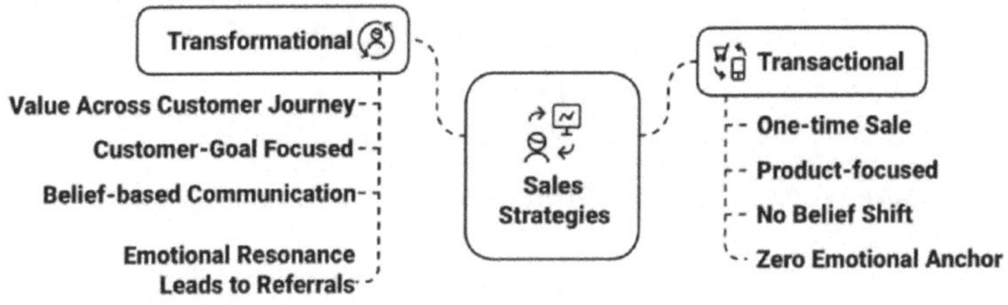

Belief Shifting With Empowering Words

From A NO to a YES: The Power of Belief-Shifting

In the year 2000, I was travelling a lot for business. Almost every week, I was in a different city. **I had a deep desire to marry one of my batchmates, but I was not in touch with her.** At that time, there were no mobile phones; **I just had her address.**

So every 10-15 days, I used to send her a postcard from a different city, with a motivational message to become

successful in achieving her dream of clearing the civil services exam.

We had never talked in the last 5 years, It was a one-sided communication of sending inspiration to her with my concern and love. I was communicating the empowering quotes to encourage her to believe in her vision, to think positively, to be disciplined, and to take massive action in the direction of her goals.

Surprisingly, I received an email from her in 2002, and I dated her for the first time in 2002. Later, we got married in 2004. It's my experience that when you inspire and help people with their growth, it changes their beliefs and perception about you.

In college, she said no to me, and then her beliefs shifted, and she chose me as her life partner.

The same works with any human being, even for our customers.

You do not need to chase your customers, you need to have the intention to help them grow in their life journey. You need to guide them with perfect solutions to their problems as well as inspire them for next-level growth. Your inspiration is that extra mile that will change their beliefs about you. Go that extra mile and you become the only choice for your customers. They start resonating with you and want to do business with you.

Chapter 5

INVISIBLE MARKETING

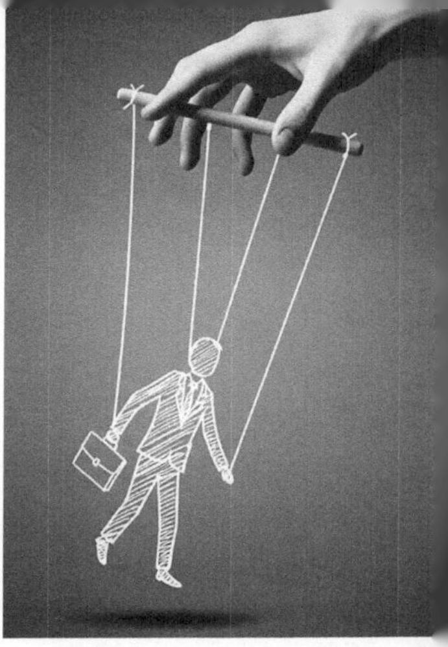

The Law of Association

To understand the powerful strategy of invisible marketing, we must first understand the law of association. Aristotle explained the psychology of the human mind, how ideas, concepts, and experiences become linked & influence learning, memory, and behavior. This means ideas that occur together in the same time & space get associated.

For example, you see - Just Do It, with the Nike Logo, you associate the empowering words with the Nike Brand.

The key to building a strong association is repetition. Repeated exposure to the same ideas or experiences strengthens the association between them. Another thing to understand is that positive ideas that give pleasure or inspiration are more likely to be remembered than those associated with pain.

When you link your brand with positivity in your customers' minds, you will be remembered and respected.

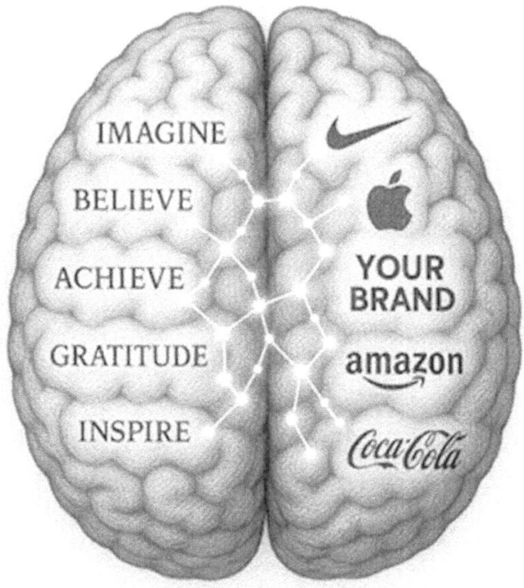

Repeatedly exposing your brand with positivity to your customers is Invisible Marketing. The marketing that is not loud and silently builds your respect and remembrance & you are at the top of their mind's recall when they need to buy the products or services that you are selling.

It plants invisible anchors in the customer's mind & they start trusting you even when they are not aware. Invisible Marketing works in the background, influencing the buying decisions at the subconscious level.

"Whatever is repeatedly linked together in the mind becomes inseparable."

It means if your customer sees some empowering words again and again alongside your brand, over time, his brain automatically links your brand with the feeling of empowerment, even without any conscious effort.

Leveraging the Law of Association with Motivational Gifts

To link your brand with empowering thoughts in the mind of your customer, you need your customers to repeatedly see empowering words & your brand together in the same space and time. Motivational Gifts are the most powerful tool to anchor your brand with positivity in the mind of your customer.

Embedding Yourself in Your Customers' Minds & Environments

Motivational Gifts create deep associations of your brand with positivity. They stay in the life of your customer for a long time & are seen repeatedly by your customers.

Your customers' desks can be the biggest real estate for invisible marketing. A useful gift with empowering words printed on it, with your bran,d will link the positive emotions of growth with your brand.

Your brand will live on their desk silently, reinforcing your presence every single day. Motivational Gifts are value-driven and carry positive emotions ...and it makes your brand become part of their environment. **For example,** if your gift is printed with empowering words - Keep growing, keep going. Every time your customer reads "Keep growing, keep going", **their identity is getting reshaped. It's silently installing an empowering belief in their mind and linking your brand with that empowering belief.**

Choosing The Motivational Gifts

The choice of a motivational gift is very important.

A Motivational Gift has 2 components.

1. An Empowering Message
2. A Useful & Unique Product for your customer on which an empowering message will be printed.

The Empowering Message

It's very important to choose the right empowering message. The empowering message must resonate with your customers' goals. For example, if you are a builder and your customer is a family looking for a new home. The message can be an affirmation - I am grateful for my perfect home that is coming to me. This message is aligned with the secret desire of the customer.

The Useful & Unique Product

Since the lady of the home is the major decision maker in buying the home, if this message is printed on a fridge magnet that is made in the shape of a house with both the image of the house as well as the affirmation - I am grateful for my perfect home that is coming to me, the lady will see the fridge magnet in kitchen multiple times a day and her mind will keep on repeating the affirmation involuntary multiple times a day. Multiple products, like coasters or home decor, can be given to this customer by the builder at different touchpoints in the customer's journey to buy a new home.

Choose the unique products so uniquely that your customer is excited to use them because of their uniqueness, as well as because of the empowering message that is resonating with their dreams.

How You Win Customer Advocacy Through Invisible Marketing

Invisible Marketing will influence decisions of your customers without appearing to sell. Your brand enters the customer's environment as a motivational gift and eventually becomes part of their thoughts, beliefs, identity & story.

This process isn't loud — it works silently without shouting, pushing, or pitching.

Here's a step-by-step process to start Invisible Marketing in your business.

Chapter 6

INVISIBLE MARKETING FOR CUSTOMERS

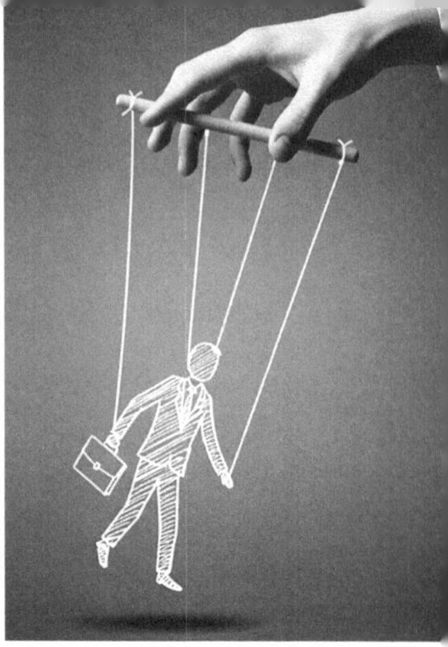

This chapter will give you the insights and strategies to implement invisible marketing both for existing customers as well as for leads, which are new prospective customers.

Invisible Marketing For Existing Customers

For existing customers, there are 4 possible ways to place your motivational gifts in their environment.

You can give them gifts.

1. Randomly
2. When they visit you or you visit them
3. When they achieve a milestone
4. Festivals

- The smartest way to Implant Belief-Shifting Motivational Gifts in Your Customer's space is strategic gifting on Key festivals with a belief-building intent.
- Making a yearly gifting calendar for existing customers is the first step, followed by crafting a motivational gift as per the festival theme.

Example of a Motivational Gifting Calendar

Festival	Month	Gift Theme	Belief to Implant	Gift Ideas
Makar Sankranti / Lohri	January	New Beginnings	Fresh starts lead to big wins.	Desk Calendar, Vision Board, 'Start Where You Are' Plaque
Republic Day	January	Patriotism & Purpose	Build with integrity. Lead with purpose.	Quote Frame with Leadership Message
Mahashivratri	March	Inner Strength	Master the mind. Master the game.	Zen-themed Desk Blocks, Spiritual Affirmation Magnet
Holi	March	Bold Action	Be fearless. Be vibrant.	Colorful Coasters with Bold Quotes
Diwali	November	Abundance & Clarity	Shine your light. Attract success.	Golden Foil Motivational Gift Box
Christmas	December	Hope & Kindness	Believe. Give. Grow.	Gratitude Gift Set, Mini Affirmation Tree

New Year	December/ January	Goal Setting & Vision	Your future is built today	Vision Cube, Affirmation Calendar

Invisible Marketing For New Customers

Invisible marketing plays a great role in new business development. When we integrate motivational gifting with key touchpoints, we create a smart customer journey.

Giving motivational gifts to your customers along with marketing materials at selected touchpoints is the smartest way of implementing Invisible Marketing. This way, you educate your customers with the right marketing materials as well as inspire them with motivational gifts. The table below gives an example of how you can integrate motivational gifting at various touchpoints.

Invisible Marketing & Touchpoints Integration

Customer Journey Stage	Touchpoint	Why Gift Here	Impact of Motivational Gift
1. Awareness	First impression (event, expo, meeting)	Creates an emotional connection early. Helps you stand out in a sea of vendors.	Builds curiosity, establishes your brand as thoughtful and value-driven.
2. Lead Nurturing	After a good conversation or follow-up	Most follow-ups are forgettable. A small gift adds surprise and emotional imprint.	Keeps you top of mind and moves the lead from cold to warm naturally.

3. Deal Milestone	Proposal sent after the negotiation call	Shows seriousness, builds rapport, and subtly anchors positivity with your brand.	Shifts perception from "vendor" to "partner."
4. Purchase Confirmation	Order placed or payment received	Celebrates the beginning of the relationship, not the end.	Triggers dopamine, reinforces trust, and increases excitement to work with you.
5. Delivery or Handover	When delivering a product/ service	Adds surprise and delight at the moment of fulfillment.	Enhances unboxing, increases satisfaction, and makes the experience memorable.
6. Success Moment	When the client achieves a win using your product/ service	Reinforces that you're part of their success journey.	Deepens emotional connection. Encourages loyalty and word-of-mouth.
7. Retention/ Renewal	Contract renewal, re-order, or anniversary	Keeps the relationship alive beyond transactions.	Reduces churn, increases LTV, and nurtures long-term partnerships.

8. Reactivation	Inactive or lapsed client	A surprising, personal gift can reignite conversations more effectively than discounts.	Break the ice. Signals you value the relationship, not just the sale.

Invisible Marketing (IM) Framework

Here is the invisible marketing framework that you can use to implement invisible marketing strategies in your business. This will help you to design your invisible marketing kits for both existing as well as new customers

Scan this QR code to get a copy of the IM framework

Chapter 7

INVISIBLE MARKETING FOR YOUR INNER CIRCLE

Your inner circle is the closest group of people who directly or indirectly contribute to your personal and business growth. They are not just resources—they are relationships.

Your Inner Circle includes:

- **Employees** – the internal team that turns vision into execution.
- **Family and close friends** who support them through highs and lows.
- **Vendors and strategic partners** – external collaborators are essential to scaling and sustaining operations.

Why is it important to nurture this inner circle?

Because this group forms the emotional and operational ecosystem of your business. When they feel inspired, seen, and valued, their energy feeds directly into your brand's performance. Your team becomes more aligned. Your family becomes more supportive. Your partners become more invested. And you stay grounded and driven.

Employees

One of my mentors said, You build your people, and those people will build your business. Your first customers are your team, your employees, who are working hard to turn your vision into reality. They're the first ones to buy into your vision. They show up when it's messy. They execute your dream. They are your brand in motion. Yet most business owners forget this. They pour crores into marketing outside, while their inside culture is starving.

Your external brand is a reflection of your internal energy. So, how do you help your team grow? Motivational Gifts are tools for culture-building. Motivational gifts are belief anchors. **When your team sees your gift on their desk that says** "Keep Growing. Keep Going.", it's not just decor — **It's a daily dose of purpose**. It's a subconscious nudge. It's an emotional link to your vision.

You're not just saying "thank you." You're saying: "You matter. Your growth matters. This mission is yours too."

You can inspire your team with motivational gifts

- Employee onboarding
- On Promotions or New Roles
- Random Acts of Recognition
- Festival or birthday gifting
- Performance milestones

When you are the source of information for them, they link their success with you and want to stay with you and your company longer. Retention is a byproduct when you are part of their growth journey in some way.

Family & Friends

Henry Ford was asked, Who is your best friend? And he answered, Anyone who brings the best out of me is my best friend. What would be a better gift than the source of inspiration when you have to gift your friends on any occasion, like a birthday, anniversary, or just random gifting?

Vendors & Strategic Partners

The relations with your vendors and strategic partners can be nurtured with thoughtful gifts. Your gifts create an impact in their life and also increase your influence. You can leverage this with

- Year-end appreciation gifts
- Strategic alliance building
- Festival gifts

Why Motivational Gifts Work

Out of sight, out of mind … its opposite is also true - When an empowering thought is in sight, it's also in mind. A well-placed quote becomes a daily anchor. It silently reinforces your relationship, your values, and your belief in the person.

Nurturing your inner circle isn't about obligation—it's about amplifying belief. And when the people around you grow with you, your business becomes unstoppable.

The most important part of your inner circle is *you*.

During my college, my mentor told me — *If you have a dream, it's your responsibility to nurture yourself to fulfill it.* I was learning from various sources how to become successful. One of the sources was **Bill Britt**, a self-made billionaire who said - You live at the level you speak. I learned the power of spoken words from him. This is what he said…

"Words are seeds. What you say to yourself will either become your prison or your breakthrough. The Bible says — A man is hanged by his own tongue."

And he wasn't the only one saying this. The same truth echoed in Sikh, Hindu, and other spiritual teachings I had come across — your inner dialogue shapes your outer reality.

Here's what I learned and started practicing, religiously, during my college years

- Speak what you want as if it's already real, and act as if you are already living that life.
- If you say I want 1 Cr Rupees, indirectly you are saying you lack 1 Cr Rupees -the statement of wanting is a statement of lack, and it will attract lack of it.
- If you say - Thank God I have 1 Cr Rupees, and say it repeatedly with emotion of gratitude, you will surely attract it, and soon it will become your reality.
- Speak your future in the present tense. Don't say "I wish I had" —start with gratitude and say "Thank God I already have it."
- How many times do you have to say it in a day? With every breath, till it becomes your mantra
- Begin everything with gratitude. Gratitude is the emotion that unlocks the energy of manifestation.

I followed this religiously and changed my self-talk. Every thought that didn't support my dream, I replaced it with a simple, affirmative statement that began with "Thank God" and declared my goal as already achieved.

In my college, I started doing affirmations to marry a girl who had no interest in me. 7 years later, in 2002, she contacted me & she was willing to marry me, but it seemed impossible to her because of an inter-caste situation.

I believed in the power of spoken words., I opened the calendar app on my phone, selected a random future date in 2004, and wrote an empowering affirmation as if it were true with gratitude. I had no clue what date, month, or time I selected.

2 Years later, as life unfolded in its surprising way, I was getting engaged to the same girl, and my phone rang — I was shocked to see the affirmation reminder in my calendar about getting engaged to her.

It hit me then — this wasn't a coincidence. It was the power of programming my subconscious mind with repeated affirmations.

I read somewhere that modern science can predict the landing of a spacecraft on the moon to a fraction of a second, and I experienced a similar experience of the manifestation of reality.

I replaced all the thoughts of desire with a statement of gratitude as if desire is a reality, and repeated it all the time in my mind like a mantra.

The universe made me experience that reality against all odds at the same time, date, and year, which I randomly selected in my mobile calendar.

Since then, I've manifested many goals — personal and professional — using this same principle. Whether it's building a business, creating impact, or developing meaningful partnerships, it always starts with the words you speak to others, but more importantly, to yourself.

Truly, you live at the level you speak.

In business and life, your most important conversation is the one you have in your own mind. Speak and live with a feeling of gratitude as if you have already accomplished your dreams and goals, and you will. But how will you speak positively about your dreams and goals if you are surrounded by negative thoughts all around?

Everything, including your TV, newspapers, social media, internet, and people around you, is bombarding you with negativity, and you are absorbing that negativity just like a passive smoker.

If people around you are smoking, even if you don't smoke, you are still damaging your body. It's the same with negativity in the environment around you.

To manifest my dreams, I created a positive environment around me, I never read newspapers, I did not have a TV in my bedroom & I did not install news channels on my TV, I read 30-minutes of a self development book everyday before sleeping, I had pictures of my dreams on my walls. I was writing every day in a diary about my future life as if it were a reality today, with feelings of gratitude, I was repeating affirmations all the time like a mantra, I even recorded affirmations and was listening to them every day. By doing all these things, I nurtured my mind with positivity.

In a nutshell, by keeping your environment positive, by repeating the empowering words repeatedly like a mantra with feelings of gratitude, you can achieve any of your goals.

In 2023, when a friend of mine asked me for a business idea, I suggested creating products with empowering affirmations and quotes that people can keep in their spaces and let those words sink deep in their subconscious with repetition.

I gave her this idea with conviction, as I have experienced the power of spoken words. For some reason, that friend did not pursue this business idea. In 2024, I thought - a good idea should not be wasted, and I decided to work on it and I launched a website, Motivationalgifts.com, a new venture was born to spread positivity with empowering words printed on products of daily use.

The purpose was to help people create a positive environment around them by integrating motivational quotes or affirmations into their day-to-day use of products. These products can rewire the mind of the person who is repeatedly absorbing the empowering thoughts around him/her. The products are categorized into Desk Accessories, Personal Use & Home Decor.

At motivationalgifts.com, all the products are crafted to inspire personal growth or to help your loved ones grow with meaningful gifting. When used in gifting, these products can enhance your marketing at any touchpoint in your customers' buying journey.

The products are categorized into 8 themes

- Empowering Affirmations
- Grateful Vibes
- Zen Mind
- Go Explore
- Productivity Pulse
- Heart Connections
- Positivity Pulse
- Inspired By

You, being the core of your organization, the most important person in your inner circle, must nurture your own mind with positive, empowering words. Your dream and vision are driving your business and your team. Just like you can't pour from an empty cup. It's important to nurture your own mindset with empowering quotes, affirmations. When you surround yourself with motivational gifts carrying the right messages, they serve as silent mentors—guiding your decisions, shaping your culture, and strengthening your leadership—every single day.

When you upgrade your office and home space with empowering quotes or affirmations

- Your space silently programs your thinking, your mind is rewired repeatedly by absorbing the empowering words.
- Motivation is contagious; when you are motivated, your energy will motivate your team and people who come in contact with you.
- When your team, family, or even visiting clients see your space charged with clarity and positivity, they feel it. It sets the tone. You become a magnet for inspiration and direction — and that's powerful leadership.
- It gives you consistency & speed, an inspiring space that unblocks your stuck state and keeps you going even on tough days.
- It works in the background at a subconscious level. The effect of empowering the environment is equivalent to reading a self-development book every day.

Chapter 8

CASE STUDIES

How These Brands Used Motivational Gifting as Invisible Marketing

Now that you've learned all about Invisible Marketing, let's see how some brands and businesses are actually using **motivational gifts** to practice it—quietly shifting beliefs, deepening trust, and creating unforgettable moments. These are not random giveaways.

These are touchpoints engineered in the buyer journey of their customers to trigger emotion, connection, and loyalty, without asking for it.

It's a step-by-step implementation to

- Map your customer journey with strategic belief-shifting gifts
- Create "Wow" touchpoints that spark referrals and repeat buying
- Position yourself as the *trusted brand* in a noisy market
- Build invisible systems that make loyalty automatic

Here are real examples of businesses across industries that integrated Motivational Gifts to create emotional impact, build recall, and deepen connections:

Ecoste

Mr Ankur Hora, who represents the brand Ecoste, is also a consultant and marketing strategist for premium real estate brands. His marketing strategy for one of his customers, Acrerise, is a perfect example of invisible marketing. They are not just selling homes, but are inspiring their customers at significant touchpoints with empowering motivational gifts.

They have made three experience-driven gift kits—each aligned with their customers' awareness stage in the buying journey: Pre-sales, Site visit, and Post-sale. But these are not just gifts. They are subtle belief-shifting tools, combining aesthetic design with meaningful affirmations to inspire the buyer's mindset.

In the pre-sales stage, the gift kit includes a Fridge Magnet, an Affirmation Cube & an Invitation letter nicely packed in a Gift box. This Box is sent to customers by courier to invite them to see the demo unit. The fridge magnet is a strategic choice as it will be seen multiple times by the family. The fridge magnet is in the shape of a home with the affirmation *"I am grateful for my perfect home that is coming to me"*. It is designed to create a positive mindset for the whole family to anticipate their dream home every day. With this gesture, the Acrerise occupies the buyer's mental space, without pushing, persuading, or pitching. When they think of their future home with positivity and gratitude, they also think of Acrerise.

At the site visit stage, the focus shifts to reassurance. After the site visit, the customer is gifted with the 2nd Box, which contains the belief-shifting marketing materials, a Book to guide the customer in their buying decisions, and motivational gifts like Coasters and a Glass Display with quotes and affirmations on abundance. Subtle messages to attract abundance in the customer's life become a part of their daily routine as they see those empowering affirmations on the gifts given by Acrerise. These empowering messages enable them to gently counter fear, indecision, and delay. Instead of follow-up calls, these gifts bring the presence of the brand to their growing mindset.

Post-sale, once a customer has made the purchase, their ideal feelings will be feelings of gratitude for their new home. Here, Acrerise builds the resonance by sending them the 3rd gift KIT, which has 6 empowering gifts. These gifts are not just home decor or products of use, but carry empowering affirmations and quotes on gratitude and peace.

One of the products is a granite slate printed with the words " Grateful for abundance that fills my home, heart, and life."A wooden plaque with daily affirmations to have peace and abundance in life. The customer's mindset as well as their relationship with Acreise are both growing every day with a spiral of positive thoughts triggered by those motivational gifts in their home.

This is invisible marketing that transforms the buyers into brand ambassadors. What Ecoste and Acrerise did differently was this: they didn't just give a gift. They gave meaning. They made their brand unforgettable—not through advertising, but by becoming part of their customers' environment, thoughts, and lives.

Overbooked Academy LLP

Akshar Yadav, who is a leading marketing coach, **emphasizes the KIT (Keep In Touch) strategy as one of the most powerful strategies.** In his buyer journey, he has integrated the StartUp Kits, Letters, as well as random inspirational gifts, to keep in touch with his customers.

In one of his live events, he gifted a beautiful wooden cube with a sequence of the getting-over-booked science. This cube in the office space of his students always reminds them of the 5-step sequence of actions to take to have an overbooked business.

This gift reinforces key ideas and keeps his message present even after the event and the course ended.

JSA Online Support Services Pvt. Ltd.

During one of their live events- ***Cash Flow Summit 2025, JSA, led by Mr. Jagmohan Singh chose to gift motivational cubes to all attendees.*** It added a thoughtful touch to the experience and helped carry the event's message into each participant's daily environment.

Thind Dental – Healthcare

Thind Dental chose to ***honor their patients through gifting***, transforming a routine service into a memorable, feel-good experience that strengthened trust and loyalty.

Infinitheism – Spiritual Organization

Infinitheism has its own brand store with *motivational gifts*. These products carry the spiritual essence and extend their message into people's lives.

Pen Down Press – Publishing

Pen Down Press uses motivational gifting as **a thoughtful way to *honor their authors and engage their readers*, turning every interaction into a moment of inspiration and strengthening their identity as a purpose-driven publisher.**

Asian Cranes – Manufacturing

By gifting their clients intentionally, Asian Cranes ***created a lasting impression beyond the transaction,*** subtly reinforcing their brand values and building goodwill within their industry network.

Crystal – Events & Exhibitions

Crystal strategically ***used motivational gifting during international events like those in Dubai,*** enhancing brand perception and leaving a lasting emotional impact on attendees and partners alike.

Gebe – Outdoor Furniture

GEBE introduced a consistent gifting practice, ***offering motivational gifts every three months to key architects who are influencers to their customers.*** This regular gesture became a way to stay connected, appreciated, and remembered, without being promotional.

TNS Network – AI Tools & Infrastructure Solutions

At one of their events, TNS Network, under the leadership of Mr. Sanjeev Jain, gifted each participant a wooden cube paper weight with useful information and qr code for AI tools for business owners. It allowed the participants to access AI tools via QR code on that wooden cube anytime in their office, and this way TNS network will stay in the minds of their customers by being in sight every day on the desk space of the business owners who attended the event.

APT Network – Business Community

APT Network uses motivational cubes as well as other meaningful gifts for their customers to create belief-shifting anchors in the events. ***These gifts create a sense of connection, spark conversations, and keep the brand values present on every member's desk.***

Hotel Anupam – Hospitality

As part of ***their Dubai property launch, Hotel Anupam gifted motivational whiteboards to selected guests***. It added a thoughtful, practical element to the opening experience and left a lasting impression tied to the brand's vision.

What Do These Brands Have in Common?

They didn't just give gifts — they used gifts as *tools of belief shifting, brand anchoring, and bonding beyond transactions.* Invisible Marketing isn't a tactic. It's a philosophy. And these brands are proof that when done right, gifting becomes your *most memorable marketing.*

You've Reached the End of This Book...

But Your Invisible Marketing Journey Truly Begins Now

You now understand how brands use belief-shifting touchpoints and thoughtful gifting to create loyal, raving fans.

Now, you have two options:

Option 1

Take everything you've learned and implement it yourself. The frameworks are in your hands. You can craft your journey, your way.

Option 2:

Let us help you do it—step by step.

Scan the QR code below to instantly access:

- The Invisible Marketing Framework – a free, ready-to-use roadmap
- A 1-on-1 consultation where we'll work with you to:

- Understand your customer journey
- Identify the belief shifts needed at each stage
- Select the right message for every touchpoint
- Curate custom gifting kits that reinforce those beliefs

We'll help you translate invisible marketing from a concept into a conversion strategy — powered by meaningfully designed gifts from **www.motivationalgifts.com**

Your brand's next breakthrough is not just in what you sell...But in what your customers believe.

Scan the code. Let's co-create your Invisible Marketing Journey.